D0805140

SINGING SAINTS

Awesome songs for teens!

Terry K. Dittmer, Editor

Copyright © 2001 Concordia Publishing House
3558 S. Jefferson Avenue, St. Louis, MO 63118-3968
Manufactured in the United States of America

1 2 3 4 5 6 7 8 9 10   10 09 08 07 06 05 04 03 02 01

SONG TITLES

2. Amazing Grace
3. As the Deer
4. Awesome God (Chorus)
5. Beautiful Savior
6. Bread of Life, Make Me Whole
7. Brothers and Sisters in Christ
8. Called to Be
9. Change My Heart, O God
10. Do Lord!: Psalm 27
11. Father, I Adore You
12. Give Thanks
13. Here I Am, Lord
14. Higher Ground
15. Holy, Holy, Holy
16. I Will Call upon the Lord
17. Jesu, Jesu, Fill Us with Your Love
18. Light of the World
19. Lord, I Lift Your Name on High
20. Make Me a Servant
21. Make Us One
22. More Precious Than Silver
23. One Name
24. Open the Eyes of My Heart
25. Peace (Father, You Are Holy)
26. Sanctuary
27. Set Your Heart in Heaven
28. Shine, Jesus, Shine
29. Shout to the Lord
30. Step by Step
31. The Lamb
32. To Him Who by the Power
33. To You, O Lord
34. What Is This Bread?
35. Yes!
36. You Are My All in All
37. You Are My Own

1

Alive

L. G.

Lloyd Garrelts

He is a-live,___ I'm thank - ful.___ The

King is a-live,___ I'm free.___ He is a-live___ I'm thank -

ful.___ The King is a-live___ in___ me.___

1 He let Him - self be put___ on a tree,___ but___
2 Je - sus said, "Go and tell___ of___ Me,"___ and___

Last time to CODA

2   Amazing Grace

John Newton, 1725–1807, alt.

NEW BRITAIN
J. Carrel and D. Clayton
Virginia Harmony, 1831

1 A - maz - ing grace! How sweet the sound That saved a wretch like me! I once was lost but now am found, Was blind but now I see!

2 The Lord has prom - ised good to me, His Word my hope se - cures; He will my shield and por - tion be As long as life en - dures.

3 Through man - y dan - gers, toils, and snares I have al - read - y come; His grace has brought me safe so far, His grace will see me home.

4 Yes, when this flesh and heart shall fail And mor - tal life shall cease, A - maz - ing grace shall then pre - vail In heav - en's joy and peace.

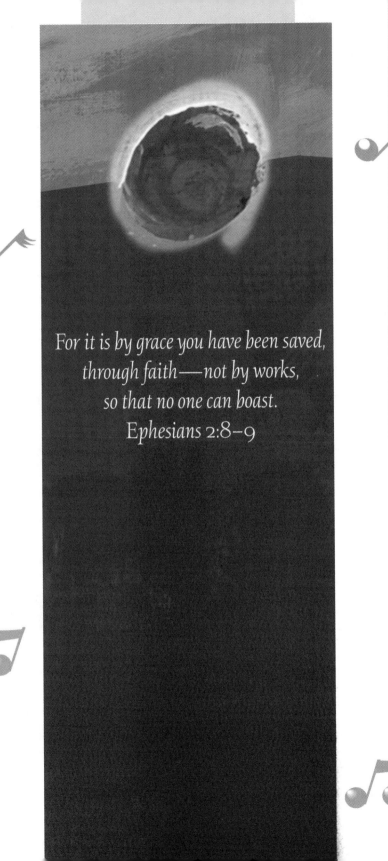

For it is by grace you have been saved,
through faith—not by works,
so that no one can boast.
Ephesians 2:8–9

3   As the Deer

M. N.

Verses

Martin Nystrom

1 As the deer pant-eth for the wa-ter, so my
2 You're my friend and You are my broth-er e-ven
3 I want You more than gold or sil-ver, on-ly

soul long-eth af - ter Thee.
though You__ are a King.
You can__ sat - is - fy.

You a - lone are my
I love You more than
You a - lone are the

heart's de-sire,__ and I long to wor - ship Thee.
an - y oth-er, so much more than an - y thing.
real joy-giv-er and the ap - ple of my eye.

4   Awesome God

R. M.

Rich Mullins

Who among the gods is like You, O LORD?
Who is like You—majestic in holiness,
awesome in glory, working wonders?
Exodus 15:11

5   Beautiful Savior

Gesangbuch, Münster, 1677
Tr. Joseph A. Seiss, 1823–1904

SCHÖNSTER HERR JESU
Silesian folk tune, 1842

1 Beau - ti - ful Sav - ior, King of cre - a - tion, Son of God and Son of Man!
2 Fair are the mead - ows, Fair are the wood - lands, Robed in flow'rs of bloom - ing spring;
3 Fair is the sun - shine, Fair is the moon - light, Bright the spar - kling stars on high;
4 Beau - ti - ful Sav - ior, Lord of the na - tions, Son of God and Son of Man!

6   Bread of Life, Make Me Whole

Mt. Olivet Lutheran Youthgroup
Plymouth, MN

7 Brothers and Sisters in Christ

T. K. D.

Terry K. Dittmer

1 Sing Al - le - lu - ia! A - men!
2 Man walked a - lone and in need,
3 Lord, teach us how to pro - claim

Let your prayers and your prais - es as -
With - out faith, hope or prom - ise or
All Your good - ness, Your love and Your

cend.
creed;
name!

Lift up your
Wan - der - ing
Lord, teach us

voic - es and sing
aim - less - ly lost
how to for - give,

to our
un - a -
and in

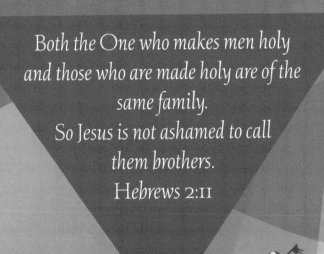

Both the One who makes men holy
and those who are made holy are of the
same family.
So Jesus is not ashamed to call
them brothers.
Hebrews 2:11

8   Called to Be

T. K. D.

Terry K. Dittmer

Change My Heart, O God

E. E.

Eddie Espinosa

Change my heart, O God, make it ev - er true; Change my heart, O God, may I be like You.

Do Lord!: Psalm 27

Traditional American
J. C. Y. (paraphrase)
Arranged by John C. Ylvisaker

Refrain

Do Lord, Oh, do Lord, Oh, do re-mem-ber me! Do Lord, Oh,

do Lord, Oh, do re-mem-ber me! Do Lord, Oh, do Lord, Oh,

do re-mem-ber me! Look a-way be-yond the blue!

Verses

1 You're my light and my sal-va-tion, I won't be a-
2 Though a host en-camp a-gainst me, I will nev-er
3 You will hide me in Your shel-ter in the day of
4 Glo-ry be to God the Fa-ther and to God the

11   Father, I Adore You

T. C.

Terrye Coelho

1 Fa - ther,
2 Je - sus, I a - dore You, Lay my life be -
3 Spir - it,

fore You. How I love You;

(May be sung as a round.)

Lord, You know all things;
You know that I love You.
John 21:17b

12   Give Thanks

H. S.

Henry Smith

13 Here I Am, Lord

Daniel Schutte
Arranged by Michael Pope, SJ, Daniel Schutte
and John Weissrock

D.S.

1 "I, the Lord of sea and sky, I have heard My
2 "I, the Lord of snow and rain, I have borne My
3 "I, the Lord of wind and flame, I will tend the

peo - ple cry. All who dwell in deep - est sin
peo - ple's pain. I have wept for love of them.
poor and lame. I will set a feast for them.

My hand will save. I, who made the
They turn a - way. I will break their
My hand will save. Fin - est bread I

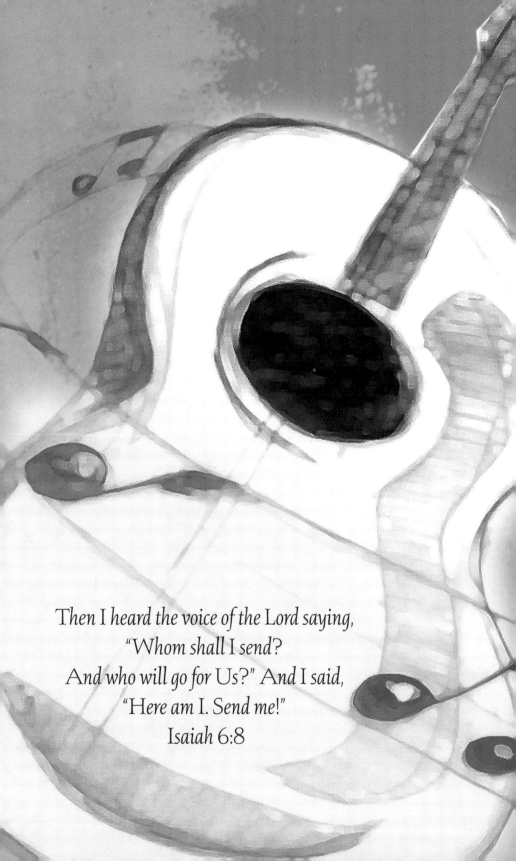

Then I heard the voice of the Lord saying,
"Whom shall I send?
And who will go for Us?" And I said,
"Here am I. Send me!"
Isaiah 6:8

14 Higher Ground

T. K. D.

Terry K. Dittmer

now each day my life be - gins With
live in love and u - ni - ty With
Trin - i - ty, the Three in One. Praise

God on the high - er ground.
Christ on the high - er ground.
God on the high - er ground.

To Refrain

Take___

15   Holy, Holy, Holy!

NICAEA

Reginald Heber, 1783–1826

John B. Dykes, 1823–76

1 Ho - ly, ho - ly, ho - ly! Lord____ God Al - might - y!
2 Ho - ly, ho - ly, ho - ly! All the saints a - dore Thee,
3 Ho - ly, ho - ly, ho - ly! Though the dark - ness hide Thee,
4 Ho - ly, ho - ly, ho - ly! Lord____ God Al - might - y

Ear - ly in the morn - ing our song shall rise to Thee.
Cast - ing down their gold - en crowns a - round the glass - y sea;
Though the eye made blind by sin Thy glo - ry may not see,
All Thy works shall praise Thy name in earth and sky and sea.

Ho - ly, ho - ly, ho - ly, mer - ci - ful and might - y!
Cher - u - bim and ser - a - phim fall - ing down be - fore Thee,
On - ly Thou art ho - ly; there is none be - side Thee,
Ho - ly, ho - ly, ho - ly, mer - ci - ful and might - y!

God in three Per - sons, bless - ed Trin - i - ty!
Which wert and art and ev - er - more shalt be.
Per - fect in pow'r, in love and pu - ri - ty.
God in three Per - sons, bless - ed Trin - i - ty!

Holy, holy, holy is the Lord God Almighty,
who was, and is, and is to come.
Revelation 4:8

16 I Will Call upon the Lord

M. O.

Michael O'Shields

17 Jesu, Jesu, Fill Us with Your Love

Tom Colvin

CHEREPONI
Northern Ghana folk melody; adapt. Tom Colvin

Ye - su,___ Ye - su,___ fill us with Your love; Show
us how to serve the neigh - bors We have from You.

1 Kneels at the feet of His friends, Si - lent - ly wash - es their
2 Neigh - bors are weal - thy and poor; Var - ied in col - or and
3 These are the ones we should serve; These are the ones we should
4 Lov - ing puts us on our knees, Si - lent - ly wash - ing their

feet, Mas - ter who acts as a slave___ to them.___
race.; Neigh - bors are near us and far___ a - way.___
love; All these are neigh - bors to us___ and You.___
feet; This is the way we should live___ with You.___

The words were written for the church in Ghana, and the traditional melody is from the church at
Chereponi. In African practice "Jesus" is usually spoken and spelled "Yesu." Because "Jesu" was used
in the early and copyrighted version of the hymn it is retained in the title. The words have been revised
to include people of every color and race.

Light of the World

18

Matthew 5:14–16

Cathy Pino

1 You are the light of the world.
2 You are a city on a hill.
3 You are a candle in the dark.
4 You are a star in the night.

You are the light of the world, ___ So ___
You are a city on a hill, ___ So ___
You are a candle in the dark, ___ So ___
You are a star in the night. ___ So ___

___ shine, ___ shine, ___ shine where you are. ___

You are the light of the world. ___
You are a city on a hill. ___
You are a candle in the dark. ___
You are a star in the night. ___

19 Lord, I Lift Your Name on High

R. F.

Rick Founds

Lord, I lift Your name on high;

Lord, I love to sing Your prais - es.

I'm so glad You're in my life;

I'm so glad You came to save us.

20   Make Me a Servant

K. W.   Kelly Willard

Make me a ser - vant, hum - ble and meek.

Lord, let me lift up those who are weak.

And may the prayer of my heart al - ways be:

Make me a ser - vant, make me a ser - vant,

make me a ser - vant to - day.

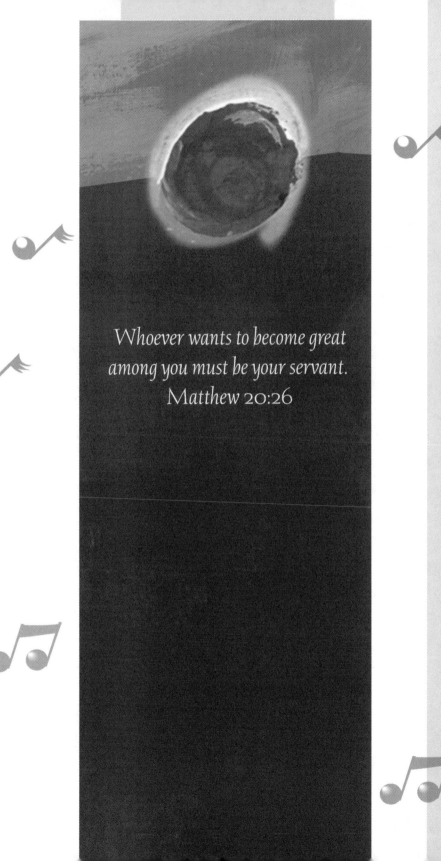

Whoever wants to become great
among you must be your servant.
Matthew 20:26

21

Make Us One

T. F.
Tim Frusti
Accompaniment arranged by Tim Frusti

As we gath - er to-geth-er in Your Son, Let us know the joy of be-ing one!___ Let the time we share in this place Be a time of love and friend-ship in Your grace. By Your Spir-it help us be One in faith and u - ni -

ty. Bless us here as we gath-er in Your Son. Give us

joy, Grant us peace, Make us one!

22　　More Precious Than Silver

L. D.

Lynn DeShazo

Lord, You are more pre - cious than sil - ver, Lord, You are more cost - ly than gold. Lord, You are more beau - ti - ful___ than dia - monds, And

noth - ing   I   de - sire   com - pares   with

1

You.

2

You.

23 One Name

Author unknown

Each section (A B C D) may be sung consecutively or simultaneously.

Salvation is found in no one else,
for there is no other name under heaven given
to men by which we must be saved.
Acts 4:12

24 Open the Eyes of My Heart

P. B.

Paul Baloche

O - pen the eyes — of my heart, — Lord,

o - pen the eyes — of my heart; — I want to

see You, — I want to

see You. —

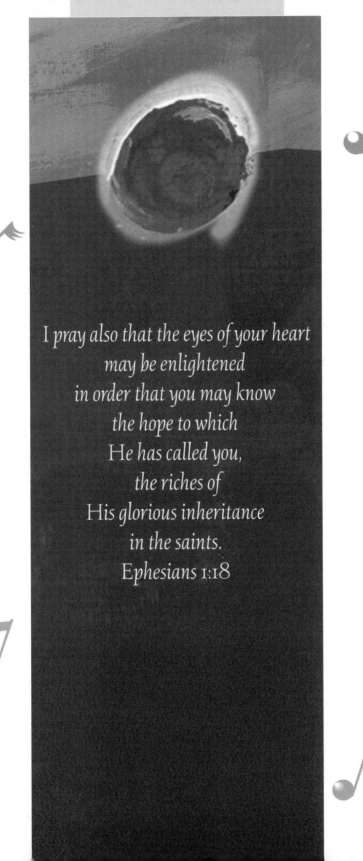

I pray also that the eyes of your heart
may be enlightened
in order that you may know
the hope to which
He has called you,
the riches of
His glorious inheritance
in the saints.
Ephesians 1:18

25   Peace (Father, You Are Holy)

L. G.

Lloyd Garrelts

26 Sanctuary

John Thompson
Randy Scruggs

J. T., R. S., HM-54

When singing in harmony, omit cue-sized notes.

27   Set Your Heart in Heaven

T. M.

Todd Miller

raised to life— in Christ,—   now set your heart— in heav-
die you come— a - live,—   so set your heart— in heav-
come to wor - ship Je - sus,   we set our hearts— in heav-

en.—   Where Je - sus rules—
en.—   It's when you serve—
en.—   The One who sanc-

1 You have been
(Voices enter 2nd time.)

28 Shine, Jesus, Shine

G. K.

Graham Kendrick

1 Lord, the light of Your love is shin - ing,
2 Lord, I come to Your awe - some pres - ence,
3 As we gaze on Your king - ly bright - ness

In the midst of the dark - ness shin - ing:
From the shad - ows in - to Your ra - di - ance;
So our fac - es dis - play Your like - ness,

Je - sus, Light of the world, shine up - on us;
By Your blood I may en - ter Your bright - ness:
Ev - er chang - ing from glo - ry to glo - ry:

Set us free by the truth You now bring us;
Search me, try me, con - sume all my dark - ness;
Mir - rored here, may our lives tell Your sto - ry;

29 Shout to the Lord

D. Z.

Darlene Zschech

Refrain

Shout to the Lord__ all the earth,__ let us sing__ pow-er and maj - es-ty, praise__ to the King;__ Moun-tains bow down__ and the seas__ will roar__ at the sound__ of Your name.__ I sing for joy__ at the work__ of Your hands,__ for - ev - er I'll love__ You, for - ev -

Tow - er of ref - uge and strength;___ Let ev-'ry breath,___ all that I am,___

___ nev - er cease to wor - ship You.

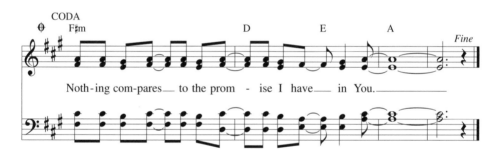

Noth-ing com-pares___ to the prom - ise I have___ in You.___

No eye has seen, no ear has heard,
no mind has conceived what
God has prepared for those
who love Him.
1 Corinthians 2:8

30 Step by Step

Beaker
Arranged by Craig Alea

The Lamb

31

G. P. C.

Gerald Patrick Coleman

1 The Lamb,— the Lamb,— O Fa - ther, where's the
2 The Lamb,— the Lamb,— One per - fect fi - nal
3 The Lamb,— the Lamb,— As way - ward sheep their
4 He sighs,— He dies,— He takes my sin and
5 He rose,— He rose,— My heart with thanks now

sac - ri - fice? Faith sees,— be - lieves— God will pro - vide the
of - fer - ing. The Lamb,— the Lamb,— Let earth' join heaven His
shep - herd kill. So still,— His will— on our be - half the
wretch - ed - ness. He lives,— for - gives,— He gives me His own
o - ver - flows. His song,— pro - long— 'Till ev - 'ry heart to

Refrain

Lamb of price!—
praise to sing.—
Law to fill.— Wor - thy is the Lamb whose death makes me His
righ - teous - ness.—
Him be - long.—

own! The Lamb— is reign-ing on His— throne!

32   To Him Who by the Power

J. C. Y.

John C. Ylvisaker

(The numbers on every two measures indicate entrances for canon singing.)

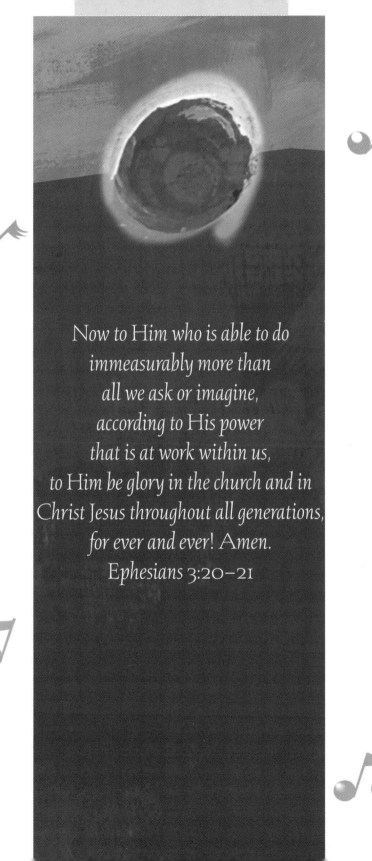

Now to Him who is able to do
immeasurably more than
all we ask or imagine,
according to His power
that is at work within us,
to Him be glory in the church and in
Christ Jesus throughout all generations,
for ever and ever! Amen.
Ephesians 3:20–21

33   To You, O Lord

Psalm 25

Krista Wiger

34   What Is This Bread?

Frederic W. Baue   Jean Neuhauser Baue

Bb/C   F   Dm   Bbmaj7

1 What is this bread?   Christ's bod - y
2 What is this wine?   The blood of
3 So who am I,   That I should
4 Yet is God here?   Oh, yes! By
5 Is this for me?   I am for -

Am7   Dm   Gm7   C   Fmaj7

ris - en from the dead: This bread we break,
Je - sus shed for mine;   The cup of grace
live and He should die   Un - der the rod.
Word and prom - ise clear.   In mouth and soul
giv - en and set free!   I do be - lieve

Bb   Bb/C   C   Bb/C   Dm   Bbmaj7

This life we take,   Was crushed to pay for our re -
Brings His em - brace   Of life and love un - til I
My God, my God,   Why have You not for - sak - en
He makes us whole—   Christ, tru - ly pres - ent in this
That I re - ceive   His ver - y bod - y and His

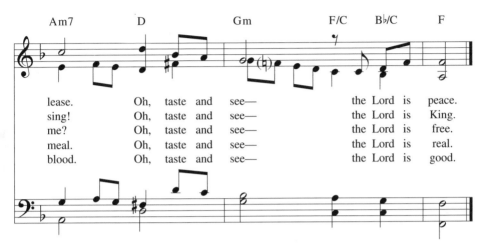

lease.	Oh,	taste	and	see—	the Lord is	peace.
sing!	Oh,	taste	and	see—	the Lord is	King.
me?	Oh,	taste	and	see—	the Lord is	free.
meal.	Oh,	taste	and	see—	the Lord is	real.
blood.	Oh,	taste	and	see—	the Lord is	good.

35

Yes!

T. K. D.

Terry K. Dittmer

36 You Are My All in All

Dennis L. Jernigan

1 You are my strength when I am weak, You are the Trea - sure that I seek. You are my All in All.

2 Seek - ing You as a pre - cious jewel, Lord, to give up I'd be a fool. You are my All in

All! Je - sus,

*Parts I and II may be sung consecutively or simultaneously.

name.   You are my All   in   All.

When I fall down, You pick me   up;   When I am dry, You fill my

cup.   You are my All   in   All!

Ending

All!

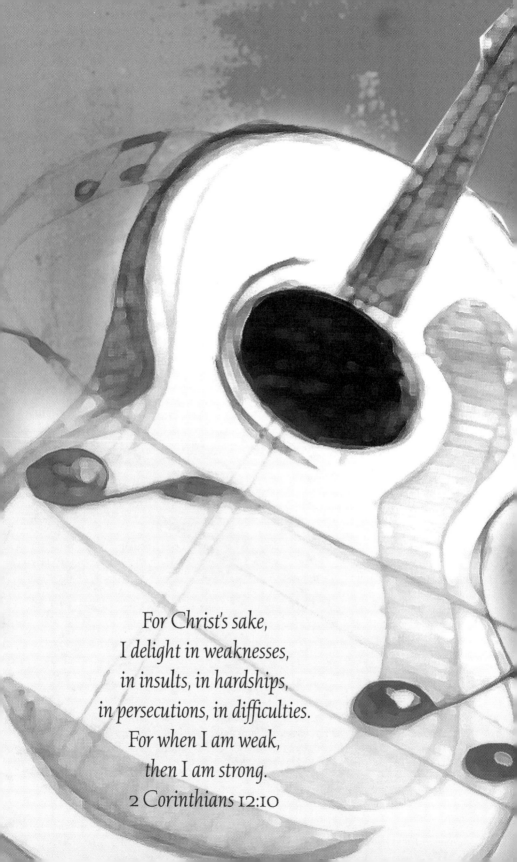

For Christ's sake,
I delight in weaknesses,
in insults, in hardships,
in persecutions, in difficulties.
For when I am weak,
then I am strong.
2 Corinthians 12:10

37 You Are My Own

G. P. C.

Gerald Patrick Coleman

1 The splash— of the wa - ter! The pow'r of the
2 To Him— you be - long— now: His grace be a -
3 Your faith— is a gra - cious Mir - a - cu - lous

Word!— The Spir - it now binds— you to Je - sus your
dored!— His grace— which sus - tains— as you grow in the
gift:— A mir - a - cle just— like His ris - ing from

Lord! And won - der of won - ders! Though by sin de -
Word! And grace of all grac - es! The vic - t'ry He
death. Both mir - a - cles , yours now In Bap - tis - m's

filed,— The Fa - ther in heav - en Now makes— you His child!
won— Is your— vic - t'ry now— through your faith— in the Son!
flood— Se - cured— by the cov - e - nant sealed— with His blood.

SCRIPTURE REFERENCES

Alive
Matthew 28:19–20
Luke 24:22–23
Philippians 2:8

Amazing Grace!
Romans 3:22–24
Ephesians 2:4–8

As the Deer
Psalm 42:1–2
Psalm 63:1–5
Psalm 84:2
Psalm 119:20, 127, 131
Psalm 143:6–7

Awesome God
Exodus 15:11
Acts 17:24

Beautiful Savior
Psalm 45:2
Revelation 15:3–4

Bread of Life, Make Me Whole
Psalm 68:4
Psalm 103:1
Psalm 145:1
John 1:29
John 6:35, 48
1 Peter 1:23

Brothers and Sisters in Christ
Hebrews 2:11

Called to Be
Romans 1:6

Change My Heart, O God
Psalm 51:10
Isaiah 64:8
Jeremiah 18:5–6
Romans 9:21

Do Lord!: Psalm 27
Psalm 27

Father, I Adore You
John 21:17b

Give Thanks
Psalm 22:3
Psalm 71:22
Psalm 100:4
Psalm 107:22
Psalm 116:17
Isaiah 12:6
Isaiah 29:19
Jonah 2:9
Luke 17:16–18
2 Corinthians 4:15
2 Corinthians 8:9
2 Corinthians 9:11, 15
2 Corinthinas 12:9–10
Ephesians 5:20
Philippians 4:6
Colossians 1:12
Colossians 2:7
Colossians 3:15–17
1 Timothy 2:1
Hebrews 13:15
James 2:5

Here I Am, Lord
1 Samuel 3:4–10
Psalm 147:14
Isaiah 6:8
Isaiah 20:24
Isaiah 65:1
Matthew 4:20–22
Matthew 5:14–16
Matthew 23:37
Luke 13:34
Romans 2:4–5

Higher Ground
Colossians 3:1–3

Holy, Holy, Holy
Exodus 33:20
Isaiah 6:2–3
Revelation 4:8–11

I Will Call upon the Lord
2 Samuel 22:47
Psalm 18:3, 46
Psalm 25:1–2, 5

Jesu, Jesu, Fill Us with Your Love
Mark 10:35
Luke 10:25–28
John 13:3-5

Light of the World
Matthew 5:14–16

Lord, I Lift Your Name on High
Psalm 71:23
Isaiah 53:9
Matthew 27:60
Mark 15:46
Luke 23:53
Acts 1:9
Romans 4:25
1 Corinthians 15:3–4
Galatians 3:13
Ephesians 4:8–10
1 Peter 2:24
1 Peter 3:18

Make Me a Servant
Ruth 1:16–17
Matthew 20:26–28
John 13:14–16
Ephesians 5:2

Make Us One
Psalm 133:1
Hebrews 10:24–25

More Precious Than Silver
Psalm 16:2
Psalm 73:25
Psalm 119:72
Proverbs 3:15
Proverbs 8:11
Matthew 13:44–46
1 Peter 1:18–19
1 Peter 2:7

Name
Acts 4:12

...en the Eyes of My Heart
Psalm 118:18
Isaiah 6:13
Matthew 13:15
Luke 24:45
Acts 26:18
2 Corinthians 4:6
Ephesians 1:18

...ce (Father, You Are Holy)
Isaiah 9:6
Isaiah 25:8
Revelation 7:17
Revelation 21:4

...ctuary
1 Corinthians 3:16

Your Heart in Heaven
Colossians 3:1–3
Hebrews 12:2

...ne, Jesus, Shine
Isaiah 60:1–3
Matthew 5:14–16
John 1:9
John 8:12
Acts 13:47
2 Corinthians 4:6
Ephesians 5:2, 8–10, 14
Philippians 2:15–16

...ut to the Lord
Joshua 21:45
Joshua 23:14
1 Kings 8:56
Psalm 31:19
Psalm 47:1
Psalm 66:1–4
Psalm 95:1
Psalm 100:1–2
Psalm 145:13
Isaiah 12:6
Isaiah 44:23

Jeremiah 33:11
Zephaniah 3:14
John 3:16
Romans 8:18, 28
1 Corinthians 2:9
James 1:12

Step by Step
Exodus 15:2b
Psalm 5:3

The Lamb
Genesis 22:7–8
Isaiah 53:6–7
Matthew 26:28, 31
John 1:29
Acts 8:32
Ephesians 1:7–8
Hebrews 9:12–14
1 Peter 1:18–19
1 Peter 2:25
Revelation 3:17–18
Revelation 4:11
Revelation 5:6, 9, 12–13
Revelation 14:1

To Him Who by the Power
Ephesians 3:20–21

To You, O Lord
Psalm 25

What Is This Bread?
Psalm 22:1
Matthew 26:26–28
Matthew 27:46
Mark 14:22–24
Mark 15:34
Luke 22:19–20
John 6:53–56
1 Corinthians 10:3–4,
    16–17
1 Corinthians 11:23–26

Yes!
Psalm 118:24
2 Corinthians 1:17–22
1 Peter 5:7-8

You Are My All in All
1 Samuel 2:8
Psalm 23:5
Psalm 116:13
Matthew 6:21
Matthew 13:44–46
Luke 12:34
John 1:29
2 Corinthians 4:7
2 Corinthians 5:21
2 Corinthians 12:9–10
Colossians 1:17
Colossians 3:11
1 Peter 2:6
Revelation 5:12

You Are My Own
Isaiah 42:6
Ephesians 2:8–10